A little book to help you through.

I hope you find something in these little pages

that helps you in some way.

With Love from J.R.T

If you're in a state of mind that isn't allowing you to be at ease it's time to pause, just for a moment and breathe.

One small moment a day can be so beneficial for you, so take a moment to be still and try to clear your mind

It's necessary..

Your mind state can affect your thoughts, your conversations, your movement, your behaviour and projections towards others, work and your lifestyle.

So just take 5 minutes..

In that 5 minutes be kind to yourself, speak Lovingly,

think Positively and simply just close your eyes and Breathe Calmly.

This will promote an opening for a positive mind set and a calm level for reacting and thinking straight.

This is a part of self-care and it is important because we often forget that it is not healthy to push too hard on ourselves, to just keep chugging along till our minds and bodies are burnt out. If we take a moment for ourselves each day it lowers the risk of shutting down and helps you to think more clearly.

Everyone talks about self-care, it's important to remember that self-care can simply be as easy as taking time for a bubble bath.

Going for a coffee with a friend and a walk in the park for a chat and fresh air.

You don't need to do anything extreme, pour a glass of wine and snuggle with a book or book a weekend away to a spa.

It's that easy, the hard part is finding the time and that's why on the first page I spoke of taking a simple 5 minutes a day for yourself.

When we feel calm within, we are able to create the happiness, love and content that we deserve.

I can't afford to have a thought in my mind

That does not feed my soul

for my greater good.

Remember to think and speak kindly to yourself.

Maintain your inner peace.

How do you relax your mind and body?

Some still struggle with this because life can be so busy, with responsibilities and jobs a mere 24hrs can pass by quicker than your lunch break.

So however you gain your calm, ensure it actually makes you happy, that every once in a while it gives you that moment to exhale.

Hobbies are good, we all need something just for us.

Write down 3 things just for you, you'd like to incorporate into your life and why, what will you believe you'll gain form them.

1.

2.

3.

Now..

♥

Go and Do at least one of these

things and make you happy.

And maybe make it a habit, Oops.. I mean Hobby!

Things get better with time.

So be Brave, be Calm, Believe in Yourself

and Don't give up.

Everything changes, having patients allows
yourself to see the good and not react negatively.

Allow yourself some room to grow,

you're best is all you can do.

And that's ok.

Peace comes in many forms.

To find it sometimes you have to give yourself

Permission to receive it first.

Some days require stillness for reflection.

And just a little extra gentleness.

Be Patient with yourself, you'll get there.

Just don't give up!

In everything we do, we try to feel

Whether it's consciously or not.

The feeling of knowing that what's being done

Has a good effect in the lives of others & the universe,

That's a feeling of accomplishment & will ripple on.

So start with you, the love you give yourself will vibrate
outward into people's lives & the atmosphere.

Patients with yourself generates kindness to all.

When we can't control what is going on in our lives

That's when we need to stop and breathe

Embrace any uncertainty

So that you can

Focus on your becoming.

Remember how diamonds are made..

Under pressure!

Often our strength rises as we go forth and things become clearer.

What I mean is, do not be afraid to go forward, we often feel we are not strong enough to handle the weight of life, work, love or even friendships.

This shows itself to us as fear or shyness, and we tend to get anxiety from these feelings, maybe even shut down and hide away. **Don't!**

Just be brave, you are stronger than you know and full of so much worth.

Each person on this earth holds a quality like no other and it is ok if you don't know what yours is. Just keep going forward, with every step your Strength, your Confidence and your Beauty will be known to you.

Courage is being shit scared..

..but saddling up anyway.

Every day comes with a gift

No.. Not the gift of life itself

The gift of a Positive lesson.

So keep your eyes open for something positive in your day

Big or small it can all make a difference.

Learn to Protect your inner peace and energy.

Treat yourself with the Honour of

Respecting and taking care of you first.

You deserve it.

+ Use the space below to list some boundaries, you can put in place to protect your peace and energy.

Be selective in your battles

Because sometimes

Peace is better than being right.

In life we can be so quick to respond, but what we should remember is not everything needs a response.

When you choose to pick your battles

you choose your inner peace and show your integrity.

Your integrity will speak volumes about your character.

Don't diminish it.

If you've made it to this page, then I want you to do one thing only today..

Think about all that you are.

Think about how far you've come.

Think about all the blessings you've received.

And feel the gratitude within you.

Sometimes you may not be feeling 100%, that's ok

please remember..

In every way and aspect of life

YOU ARE ENOUGH.

You got this.

Use the space to write some words of
encouragement to yourself.

Go ahead, Be Kind.

We can only learn from the past, I know sometimes thinking back it may cause pain, irritation, disappointment or even embarrassment..

But don't allow yourself to get hooked to the past, because it can rob you of the Positive Energy needed to face and create the Future.

Repeat:

Thou shall not break my spirit

For I am stronger then I look.

❤

Smile and laugh freely

Believe you are enough

You go ahead & love yourself

Deserve all your heart desires

Joy isn't as far as you think

The last few page is for you, write down something you want to move forward to, something you want to build within yourself, self-affirmation

Or simply just goals to achieve or build on.

Set you goals and build on them..

Be sure to be clear when you write it down

Positive intent, positive results.

A Candle loses nothing by lighting another Candle.

As you work on yourself
remember to pay forward the light you have found,
so that another who may be in need
can find their self too.
Kindness also comes in a form of knowledge.

If you have this knowledge, share.

Sometimes we have to break to find ourselves

And sometimes finding ourselves

is as easy as breathing air.

But the most amazing part is

learning how to keep your peace

Once you know

you become unbreakable.

Take care of you. x

✦

This page is simply for you to write down what

You're Thankful for, so it is visible to you

The blessings you hold in life.

Printed in Great Britain
by Amazon